Three Absolutely Necessary, Always Present Skills of an Effective, Successful Leader

Every Successful Leader Has Them…Even If They Cannot Tell You What They Are

Jack Dunigan

www.jackdunigan.com

LifeM... orida

com

C000162308

This book contains information from many sources and gathered from many personal experiences. It is published for general reference and is not intended to be a substitute for independent verification by readers when necessary and appropriate. The book is sold with the understanding that neither the author nor the publisher is engaged in rendering any legal, psychological, or accounting advice. The publisher and author disclaim any personal liability, directly or indirectly, for any advice or information presented within. Although the author and publisher have prepared this manuscript with utmost care and diligence and have made every effort to ensure the accuracy and completeness of the information contained within, we assume no responsibility for errors, inaccuracies, omissions, or inconsistencies.

ATTENTION: Quantity discounts are available to your company, organization, business, or institution.

Copyright © 2012 Jack Dunigan
All rights reserved.
ISBN: 1470132184
ISBN-13: 978-1470132187

This book is dedicated to my son, Nathaniel Dunigan, one of the most effective leaders I know.

The Three Absolutely Necessary, Always Present Skills of an Effective, Successful Leader

In the following pages I have taken nearly four decades of learning and experience, and distilled down the lessons learned, sometimes painfully, into those fundamental and basic principles upon which effective leadership is built. In those four decades I served as a trainer and consultant to many, many businesses and organizations. I founded and owned businesses myself, and did a great deal of writing along the way. This book is but one of a series on practical leadership.

Leadership is not easily defined, but it is easily identified. Ineffective leadership is quite easily seen because it is so prevalent. Simply because people find themselves in a position of responsibility and authority it does not automatically imply they possess the necessary gifts and talents for carrying out their responsibility and authority as a leader. Nor does it mean they will be an effective leader.

Most people fancy themselves to be leaders and, in one sense, nearly everybody leads someone. Mothers may be the best examples of leadership on the planet. Few have ever studied leadership principles and practices yet just about all of them do it very well. That may be because the inherent gifts come along with the gender and the role of motherhood.

I am confident that leadership as a subject can be taught. I am not confident that everyone can do it well. Some personalities simply are not suited for the responsibility. Others just don't have the gifts to exercise it beyond a limited sphere of influence.

I am certain, however, that my years of study and experience have revealed and verified that there are three absolutely essential, must have, never fail, always present skills upon which all successful, effective leadership is built. *Every successful leader does them well...even if they can't tell you what they are.*

Within the next several pages I will reveal those three fundamental gifts, define them, explain how they manifest themselves, and illuminate the evidences of their presence. Please read on. I welcome your comments. Email them to me at *comments@thepracticalleader.com*

Jack Dunigan

Practical Leadership

Other titles in this series include:

- ➢ **What You See Is What You Get - Great Leaders See The End From The Beginning**

- ➢ **How To Light A Fire Under Almost Anyone Without Getting Burned**

- ➢ **Gold All Over The Floor – How to Tap Into The Most Valuable Asset In Your Company or Organization**

- ➢ **The One Key Truth That Can Revolutionize Your Success As A Leader**

- ➢ **How To Develop Capable People**

- ➢ **How To Be A Stand Up Person In A Stoop To Anything World**

And more

Who is Jack Dunigan?

 I am a practical guy and have little patience for conceptualizing. If a concept cannot be readily and expediently translated into an action that produces desirable results, I don't bother with it. **The Practical Leader,** my blog and website, is dedicated to and focused upon practical advice for leaders and managers of businesses, corporations, non-profit agencies, families, organizations, departments, anywhere and anytime a person leads others.

I founded and directed Leadership Ministries, a non-profit agency giving practical advice to the leaders and managers of non-profits in eleven countries. The business arm of that was called The Dynamics Group and I served as consultant with clients of all types and in varied fields from the Office of the

President of the Navajo Nation to the Thousand Trails Campgrounds. I took a break from the demanding travel that consulting required to start and successfully run a custom millwork business on St. Croix in the US Virgin Islands. When I sold the business in 2009 it was rated by AllBusiness.com as #3 top employer and #4 top woodworking company by sales in the islands.

The important thing is I can unapologetically say I know what I am writing about. Yes, I have a Master's Degree. But the highest proof is in the fruit of my life. Practical Leadership works in real life!

You may already be familiar with my writings from my blogs. I author and contribute to several, but the blog to which this piece is directly connected is **ThePracticalLeader.com**.

The Three Absolutely Necessary, Always Present Skills of an Effective, Successful Leader

Every Successful Leader Has Them…Even If They Can't Tell You What They Are

Table of Contents

LEADERSHIP BY PRINCIPLE

Point your browser to Amazon.com or any comprehensive on-line book seller and type in Leadership, then select books and click go. Find the best books available on the subject. Go ahead. Take your pick. But it might take some time. There are over 360,000 possible choices in Amazon! They represent the best, and the worst, instruction on leadership available today.

I have read a good many of these books listed on Amazon, sat in a number of seminars and classes on the subject, and held positions in leadership both formal and informal for nearly forty years.

Leadership is both complex and straightforward. It is complicated to explain but simple to observe. Its principles and practices derive from complex dynamics and human relationships but it is surprisingly simple to lead once those dynamics are understood. We readily respond to effective leadership, but are confused and confounded by it when it is poorly executed.

Early in my career I spent a number of years on the Navajo Reservation in Northern Arizona. While working as a consultant to leaders in various positions of responsibility in the tribal government (from the Tourism office to the Office of the Tribal President) and in a number of charities that served the needs of the developing economy, I discovered that there is not a word in the Navajo language for "leader". The closest word commonly used is "orator."

"Leaders" in the Navajo culture and system of getting things done are talented speakers. They possess the capacity to move their constituents to action by what they say. Essentially this is true of all leaders.

Therefore the point is leadership is not actually a dedicated science, nor is it strictly an art. The concept of orator as leader actually does work. But the orator/leader cannot just say anything about any subject and earn the badge. They cannot climb to a position of respect, or remain there for long, by simply speaking well. Leaders must speak eloquently and knowledgeably about the right things at the right time in the right way then follow through with an ability to get things done.

Now, you might be wondering just when I am going to get to the *Three Absolutely Necessary, Always Present Skills Of An Effective, Successful Leader.* And you might even be more perplexed when I tell you oratory skill is not one of them! But it isn't. That and other layers of skills I will examine and define in my blog and courses but they are not one of the three essential skills I will reveal. You may know some of them, and probably perform them admirably even if you can't name them. Speaking well is an essential skill but it is *not* one of the 3 absolutely essential skills simply because one must be certain what one says. There are skills that underpin that of speaking.

After years of formal education and many more years of real life experience, through countless consultations with leaders effective and ineffective, I have processed down and through the many leadership capabilities and defined my own list of *Three Absolutely Necessary, Always Present Skills Of An Effective, Successful Leader*.

This is about the place that a quote from an authority on leadership is inserted. Well, I won't disappoint. Without apology I will notify you now that I will from time to time, use references to the Bible along with other references to literature both recent and classic, in my books and blogs. Of one thing I am certain; principles apply in every era, in every culture, and across language barriers. They were true yesterday, true today, and will be true tomorrow. They are true here, true there, and true beyond. In fact, the test of a valid leadership principle is its universal application.

> *The principles of effective leadership are UNIVERSAL!*

So references to any body of literature have their place inasmuch as we can extract from them universal principles by which we can direct our intentions, order our lives, and measure our progress.

They are the truths upon which effective practices are built. A solid leadership experience must have a solid foundation. Effective leadership must be built on truths proven in real life, refined by challenge, and tempered by experience. They are not theoretical. They do not emerge from academia except that analysts have identified their use in real life. If you build and implement your

> *The principles of effective leadership are* **FOUNDATIONAL!**

leadership practices based on techniques without understanding the principles which birthed them, your effectiveness will be limited to a specific setting or culture. Practices that work in the board room do not necessarily translate well to the shop floor, but the *principles* that spawned them do.

So, here's the quote.

*"AND OF THE SONS OF ISSACHAR, MEN WHO **UNDERSTOOD THE TIMES**, WITH **KNOWLEDGE OF WHAT ISRAEL SHOULD DO**, THEIR CHIEFS WERE*

*TWO HUNDRED; AND ALL THEIR KINSMEN WERE **AT THEIR COMMAND**." 1 CHRONICLES 12:32*

This reference illustrates the writer's ability to discern just what sets apart the leaders (chiefs) of this particular group. By recording his observations, the writer has defined fundamental, foundational, effective leadership. There is nothing esoteric here. The three skills are unusual in the sense that they are so ordinary, so nondescript, so pedestrian, yet so very effective!

To put these ancient words into a modern setting, consider this:

The morning broke bright, sunny, and clear. It promised to be a glorious day in New York. September days have that crisp feel and sharp contrast that means summer has passed and colorful autumn days will buffer the oncoming winter. But within a few hours the routine of the city would be horribly disrupted, pulling the attention of the entire world into downtown Manhattan. In the chaos and anarchy that followed the attack on the World Trade Towers and their collapse, one person stood out as an example of effective leadership.

Mayor Rudy Giuliani's performance that morning perfectly demonstrates all three foundational skills of successful, effective leadership.

1. He demonstrated a complete grasp of the "times." He quickly got a handle on exactly what was going on even while it was still happening.
2. He knew what to do next, and what to do after that, and what to do after that...
3. And he was able to marshal the resources and people to make those things happen.

Within minutes of the first attack Giuliani was on the scene and taking charge.

> ➤ *The person with ideas and the ability to put them into practice is engaged in leadership and moving toward greater spheres of influence.*

> ➤ *The person with few ideas and limited ability is disengaged from leadership and moving away from greater spheres of influence.*

> ➤ *The person with no ideas but possessing some ability will inevitably work for a leader.*

TAKEAWAYS

- ✓ Oratory skills are important, at times critical, but they are not one of the three essential skills.
- ✓ The principles upon which effective leadership are founded were true yesterday, true today, and will be true tomorrow.
- ✓ The three skills are unusual in the sense that they are so ordinary, so nondescript, so pedestrian, yet so very effective!
- ✓ Know what's going on.
- ✓ Know what to do next.
- ✓ Be able to take action and get others to act as well.

Skill #1 - Understand the Times

You just have to know what's going on while it is going on. You have to have some grasp of why it is happening, and you need to understand the implications of what it means for you and your team! You cannot get where you want to go if you do not know where *you are*! You cannot offer guidance and direction unless you know where you are and have some idea of how to get from here to there. Of course, you could say anyone could see what was going on when the Towers fell. But I dispute this is so.

Take, for example, the lack of Federal leadership after the Deepwater Horizon explosion and oil spill. At neither the city nor the State level did they "get it" in the former nor at the Federal level in the latter. The resulting chaos and tragedy only underscores the reality of people in charge who were clueless about the situation on the ground.

You cannot effectively address a situation if you do not know the conditions which presently exist and the general mood of the group! In takes genuine skill to be able to see the big picture and all the little scenes that make up the big picture.

It is not always important to know, at the moment of discovery, why something happened. In order to be effective, Mayor Giuliani did not need to know *why* the planes crashed into the towers. It was, however, imperative to know *what* has happened... and what *is* happening. There will be time for examination of motives and intentions later. Your concern as leader is to understand the times so you can determine what to do.

Effective leaders are able to simplify complex circumstances, to comprehend a broad range of events and digest them into simple, easier-to-handle components. Leaders must be capable of cutting through the fog, living above the fray, maneuvering around the obstacles. While this skill is particularly acute in times of crisis, it is a skill universally applicable. The principle at work here is called **"Line of Sight"** and you can read more about it on my blog (www.thepracticalleader.com). In a gist, it says that the higher up the organizational ladder, the farther and broader your range of vision. You have to have two kinds of "sight":

Insight – the ability to discern the dynamics of any given situation, setting, opportunity, and group.

and

Outsight – the vision to see the end from the beginning...and the steps in between.

Insight is the capacity to see into a situation, behind the obvious, and underneath the apparent. The ability to be in the know seems to be more inherent and innate than it is acquired. I have observed that while there are techniques one can employ to enhance understanding, you either are an observant discerning person or you are not. However, you would not be reading this unless you have a desire to enhance your leadership ability or have questions about effective leadership. Therefore I can assure you that you possess the basic component of an understanding person – curiosity.

Curiosity is the motivation to know more than the obvious. It is to wonder what's happening and why. Inquisitive people determine to discover actions and reasons. They seldom accept things as they are. They are keen students and learners of the intricacies of human nature. They understand the effect culture, custom, personality, and conditioning have on the actions of individuals and groups.

In my work with the Navajo Nation I often trained non-Navajos in the skills of cross-cultural communication. I emphasized that Navajos are, by and large, a more cooperative culture than they are competitive. A teacher in one of my classes told me that when she used games in class as a teaching tool, she noticed almost everyone "won" at the same time. At first she thought it remarkable that every student was learning at the same rate. Then she discovered that the first to complete an activity would wait until the others were done so that everyone would win together. It was culturally unacceptable that one person would stand out among the others.

Insightful leaders are quite capable people and situation readers. It may include body language, but there is more to it. Reading people and situations is a lot like reading a book. Individual words make up sentences. Individual sentences make up paragraphs. Paragraphs lumped together make up chapters. Chapters assembled in order make up a story. So it is with reading people.

Small, individual actions and comments work together to convey a thought or idea to you of who the person really is. Several actions and comments assembled together to make up a behavioral trend or trait. Traits and trends assembled together betray character and communicate to you a more complete picture of what someone is like, how they think, and help you to predict how they will behave. When the observer, meaning you, reads a person through the lens of experience, education, and wisdom, you can understand them. When you understand them, you can understand what they will do, or not do, in any particular situation. When you understand this, and you understand the situation and circumstances, you have mastered skill number one.

Reading the situation or circumstances is, in principle, the same as reading a person. Individual, sometime isolated incidents make up a bigger story. The

> *Intuition is a combination of historical (empirical) data, deep and heightened observation and an ability to cut through the thickness of surface reality. Intuition is like a slow motion machine that captures data instantaneously and hits you like a ton of bricks. Intuition is a knowing, a sensing that is beyond conscious understanding ---- a gut feeling. Intuition is not pseudo-science.*
>
> *Abella Arthur*

ability to understand what's going on is the capacity to gather small pieces of information, carefully and logically combine them into a larger set of facts and intuitions, deduce the dynamics at play all without jumping to conclusions.

You use your powers of observation to, well, observe. You can "see" what's going on and can, should someone ask "What's going on here?" you can answer them.

It is a fine blend of science and art. It is not Tarot cards, fortune telling, or palm reading. It is the power of acute observation and deduction melded with a sense of knowing. It is sometimes called *intellection*. In some circles you will hear the term *discernment* – the quality of being able to grasp and comprehend what is obscure. The emphasis here is upon accuracy. Insight and understanding are not playing hunches or wild guesses but they yield the confident knowledge of what's really going on based on keen powers of observation tempered by wisdom and experience which has made the leader sensitive and intuitive. This skill enables you the leader to comprehend the dynamics at work and the effects of those dynamics so you can make the right decision and do the right thing.

Leaders with "outsight" possess a talent for process and organization. They can put plans into place, see the sequences needed to achieve objectives, understand where to begin and foresee where their actions will lead. I explore this topic in more exhaustively in my book *"What You See Is What You Get – Great Leaders See The End From The Beginning,"* but here is a shorter synopsis.

Managers follow processes with little or no responsibility to consider the results of their actions. Effective leaders have many of the same skills of winning chess players. They can see the possibilities, understand the results one action will make on the bigger picture, and weigh the consequences. They are, in a real sense, far-sighted. Short-sightedness will often yield temporary and apparent success. It will, however, most often lead to serious issues later. Many failed businesses succumbed to the seduction of bigger total sales numbers without considering whether those sales numbers came at the expense of margin. They forget, or ignore, the ultimate imperative of the bottom line. Outsight would have pointed out the flaw in this strategy, revealing that short-term gains at the expense of margin will ultimately lead to long-term losses.

Outsight is one of the key components that separate leaders from managers. Managers oversee processes. Leaders gather all the many processes together into one comprehensive strategy. Managers may know a step or two, but leaders build the path to the final product.

Outsightedness is often the product of experience and position. Experienced leaders understand how one event or set of circumstances will impact another. They know something about human nature, about conditions and events within organizational structures, and can predict what will most likely happen.

Hand in hand with that is the position one occupies within an organization. The higher up you climb the farther you can see. In nature this is a product of natural sight. In leadership it is too. You can see what's going on. It is also the product of a sixth sense, an intuition that not only senses what is going on within group or organizational dynamics but senses what the outcome will be.

Further, *outsighted* leaders "see" where they want to go. They can conceptualize and articulate vision. This again distinguishes leaders from managers.

Six Differences between Effective Leaders and Managers

First, effective leaders think longer term while managers are unit thinkers. Managers process steps, checklists, charts, systems, and diagrams. Please don't think I am maligning managers. Managers are absolutely and comprehensively necessary to the efficient function of a group. But their responsibilities are different. Managers exercise leadership to some degree but of necessity limit themselves to units of time, quantities of product, and/or scheduling of events. Leaders, at least the effective ones, have a knack for considering the long-term effects of the processes managers must manage.

Second, effective leaders look beyond the unit they are heading and grasp its relationship to larger realities. They are able to connect the pieces and see how one unit plays into another then joins with yet another to create the desired result. Managers continue to focus their attention upon processes even if those processes no longer contribute to the end objectives or their validity has been lost.

When I lived and worked in the Caribbean, I learned that it took a great deal of effort to get a driver's license. There were endless papers that had to be completed, medical exams that had to be passed, and you had to find someone to take two passport-size photos so the license bureau could laminate them into your license. The island government finally decided to join the modern world and purchased computerized equipment that enabled them to take a photo at the window and produce a driver's license on the spot. For many months following the introduction of these machines, applicants still had to bring with them two passport size photos. Clerks would collect the photos and staple them to the application, then ask the applicant to stand still while his or her photo was taken by the computer for the license. Finally someone asked why two passport photos were still required when the computer took the license photo? The response? "Because it is on the checklist and the manager says we have to follow the list!"

Third, effective leaders reach and influence constituents beyond their jurisdictions. Managers are limited by geography and focus to their particular place in the organizational plan. Leader's see up and out, but manager's focus down and within. The effects of effective leadership are usually far-reaching. Decisions and supporting actions change the nature of business, politics, culture, and life. Managers, on the other hand, are committed to keeping systems running as they are. When leaders lead they build recognition. Their renown spreads. Others see what they've done or hear about it and success promotes emulation.

This is the "tide effect." When the tide rises, all boats float higher (unless they're chained to the ocean floor – more about this subject can be found in my book *"How to Light a Fire Under Almost Anyone Without Getting Burned"* which is part of the Effective Leadership Series). Effective leaders bring success to everyone in the group, to any associated groups within the company or organization, and to some extent, to the competition in business. How?

Departments win or lose as units. Companies succeed or fail entirely. Along the way, those leaders responsible for segments of the operation can inspire others to action.

Competition provokes imitation. When another's group does better than ours, we are prompted to overtake them. The reverse is true, too. When my company does well my competitors don't just roll over and give up. They respond by improving. Look at McDonalds and its many imitators. Burger King, Wendy's, Arby's, and more continually practice one-upmanship. McDonalds set the standard and they keep raising the bar. Apple Computers does the same.

Fourth, effective leaders put heavy emphasis on the intangibles of vision, values, and motivation. They understand the non-rational and unconscious elements that characterize and influence interaction between leaders and their constituents. This is where leaders really shine. They don't have to be very specific. Painting with a broad brush attracts the widest audience. Followers love to hear of grand and sweeping vistas yet to be realized. Presidents Reagan and Obama were very gifted at this. They both spoke in terms that resonated with listeners but avoided being very specific which allowed those listeners to draw their own conclusions about what the speaker was promising. That the interpretations might have had little to do with what the leader could actually do was, at the point of speaking, irrelevant. It is the very act of inspiration that matters. Managers usually don't even attempt to do this. They just get through the day getting the task list completed.

Fifth, effective leaders have the political skill to cope with conflicting requirements of multiple constituencies. I confess that is much easier said than done. Leaders are a great deal like kings or queens trying to unify heretofore competitive fiefdoms so as to join them together to participate in a *common vision*. Lee Iacocca reported that the condition that nearly brought the Chrysler Corporation to ruin was competing constituencies within. While it is critical that leaders focuses forward and outward, failure to pay attention within may render their entire visionary acumen meaningless. Conversely, it is the skill of the leader in selling his/her vision that can unite competitors and turn efforts toward the future. Inability to inspire and unite, or the refusal of constituents to participate in your vision as leader while pursuing their own vision is to permit, perhaps even promote two (or more) visions. This is di-vision, the condition wherein attention and effort is incapable of focus. Division will destroy any company or organization. I address this very critical skill in my book *"What You See is What You Get."*

Sixth, effective leaders think in terms of renewal. Managers, by virtue of their role and responsibilities, are like maintainers. They oil the machinery of organization and operation keeping its schedules and procedures running smoothly. They tend to become protective of those schedules and procedures and consequently resist change. Leaders understand the times and know that the times always change. History is cluttered with the bones of once glorious nations, companies, and organizations that simply failed to adapt to changing times. Renewal is not a fresh coat of paint. Renewal is to make new, not just makeover the old.

I need to say one more thing about this subject. I've discussed that capacity of sensitivity that enables a leader to discern present circumstances. On a broader scale, there is the concept defined in the first chapter – "understanding the times."

We are all victims of and shapers of the times in which we live. Generational differences shape the way we live and the way we look at the way we live. In my book *"How to Light a Fire Under Almost Anyone"* I explore this subject in much greater depth. But here, I can afford the space to merely address it.

The premise upon which the three essential skills are built and the target toward which they are directed is the accomplishment of some objective which has been determined by circumstances and needs. You as a leader want to accomplish something with importance and value determined by a large set of conditions and circumstances.

The "times" as I define it here includes the culture which gave birth to and shaped the attitudes, ideas, values, and ambitions, and ethics of the people who make up the group you are leading. The behavior of those you lead, which includes their ability to understand what you are after, how it is to be accomplished, why they should cooperate, and to what extent they will respond to your leadership will determine your success or failure. That behavior will be shaped and immediately influenced by the times. Previously in this chapter I addressed the immediate times but it would be a mistake to neglect the times in general.

If your group includes those who belong to a different generation or generations, your task will be more complicated. Perhaps the greatest challenge will come in the realm of motivation. The readiness with which subordinates will respond, the intensity by which they will labor, and the reason(s) under which they will validate their participation will all be influenced by the "times" in which you, and they live. Motivation and response is a comprehensive subject, one which I address thoroughly in *"How To Light A Fire Under Almost Anyone Without Getting Burned."*

<u>TAKEAWAYS</u>

- ✓ If you don't know where you are, you cannot readily find your way forward.
- ✓ Discerning people have a knack for seeing the dynamics that are at work in any circumstance.
- ✓ Leadership and management are not the same things.
- ✓ The two dimensions of vision, in this setting, are insight and outsight.
- ✓ The times in which you lead mean not only the immediate circumstances demanding your participation but the larger set of dynamics that influence the response in those you lead...and how you lead them.

SKILL #2 - KNOW WHAT TO DO NEXT

Michael Vance, creative consultant for Walt Disney, tells this story.

One late summer night, he was walking down Main Street USA in Disneyland in Anaheim, California. It had been a busy day and the street was filled with guests making their way to the exits. At the same time, a team of draft horses that pull the trolleys up and down Main Street had been unharnessed. The horses had been working for quite some time and were fatigued. Their handler chose to take the horses straight down through the crowds instead of out through one of the many service exits strategically placed between buildings. Theme parks all have many "hidden" doors and gates to move employees and goods in and out.

The danger was both immediate and imminent. Large tired animals and irritable crowds do not mix. As the handler tried to move the team of horses through the crowd, a supervisor came upon the scene. In a sharp voice and with decisive movements, he began speaking. "Let's get these animals out of here! Come on, move them over this way! Over here! Over here!"

He was decisive, sharp, insistent, and loud. One would think he was angry and upset over the lack of wisdom displayed by the horse's handler. No sooner had they moved the horses through an exit and closed the gate behind them, did the supervisor turn to him and say, in a calm but authoritative voice, "Alright, now as soon as you fellas take these horses back to the pony farm, come up to my office and let's talk about what's happened."

He then proceeded to explain the danger, the dynamics as it were, that existed in the situation just handled, and what to do about it in the future. Once again, all *Three Absolutely Necessary, Always Present Skills Of An Effective, Successful Leader* are clearly demonstrated here. The leader, in this case a shift supervisor:

✓ *Understood the times* – he saw the situation clearly even when the team handler could not. He understood the "times" in that it was a volatile situation with an explosive combination of fatigued horses and impatient people.

✓ *Knew what to do next* – this was not the time to assemble a focus group and analyze the potential outcomes should the circumstances remain unchanged. It was time for action and the supervisor knew it. He knew why it was important to do that exact thing at that precise moment. He knew that the likelihood for violent chaos grew exponentially with each passing second. He knew that firm and quick action had to be taken to avoid injury to innocent people.

✓ *Was able to command people to make it happen.* The combination of his office as supervisor AND his manner of dealing with the situation would and did produce the desired response.

When the horses had been moved away from the crowds and into a place of quiet and safety, he, the supervisor:

✓ *Understood the times* – the crisis was over, there was no need for sharp, quick action. So he turned to the handler and quietly said,

"Alright, now let's talk about what just happened."

✓ *Knew what to do next* – a sharp rebuke was not called for here, not even a reprimand. His history with the handler assured him the handler was ignorant, not remiss. This was the time for education not reprisal. The supervisor understood that the best time for education is usually at the point of failure. He was able to discuss with the handler what happened, why it happened, why it should not happen again, and what to do about it in the future.

✓ *Was able to command people to make it happen* – his role as leader demanded he do something. He could not just walk away. Thus his role as supervisor gave him the platform to deal with the situation and underscore what future actions would be required of the handler.

Douglas MacGregor has advanced a theory of leadership that has become quite well established. He calls it X & Y leadership. His focus is on the prevailing attitude and demeanor of the leader. X leaders are autocratic, issue orders, and generally lead from the top down. Y leaders are participative leaders gathering a consensus before proceeding.

I propose that the best, the most effective leaders are both. Actually, they are able to assume the manner of both. In the example cited just now, that supervisor manifested both X & Y leadership.

➢ One of the most critical decisions a leader faces is which approach to take. While I address this very critical topic in much greater depth in my book *Gold All Over The Floor* –

How to Tap Into The Most Valuable Asset In Your Company or Organization, I do want to make the following distinction now.

Y style leadership generally deals with and addresses *causes*.

X style leadership generally deals with and addresses *effects*.

In the account of the horses at Disneyland, the supervisor employed X style leadership when he took charge, began issuing orders, and directly interfered in the situation. As soon as the critical moment had passed and the horses had been removed from the crowds, he switched to Y style so he could address the cause, engaging those he supervised in a discussion so as to determine the reasons behind what happened and what to do about. There are many, many times in a leader's experience when both (and combinations thereof, are required.

The most effective leaders understand the "times." They know what style to use, when to use it, and are quite adept at moving between the two (and its several variations).

General McLellan was President Lincoln's first choice to lead the Union army against Confederate forces. McLellan was a terrific organizer, a great logistics man. His main vulnerability was that he could not muster the will to fight. He was a man of planning and organization but not of action. He just could not garner the inner resources to overcome inaction. Inaction manifests an inertia-like quality. It resists change in motion and direction. If inaction continues long enough, it can destroy an army's will to fight, even to survive. This principle applies equally well in business and organizations – they will eventually fail.

Consequences of INACTION

✓ *Provokes doubt* – he who hesitates may not be lost but he certainly will lose momentum and wonder why. Failure to act always provokes questions. You may be certain those questions will ultimately be directed to and aimed at you. Everyone knows leaders are supposed to produce and are paid to produce. Ultimately those who work for you and those for whom you work will not excuse you because of rough water – *they will expect you to bring the boat in.*

✓ *Contributes to confusion* – once doubt has a foothold, the lack of answers will lead to confusion about the role of the worker(s) and the leadership. This will especially happen if someone else, someone other than you, prescribes action.

✓ *The McLellan Syndrome sets in* – the will to act wanes, seriously. Now even more effort will be required to get off the dime and get something done. You know the axiom – Lead, Follow, or Get out of the way.

✓ *Failure to achieve breeds failure to try* – inertia can be fatal. Gone on long enough, inaction causes the collective "muscle" of your work force to atrophy.

General Ulysses S. Grant was a failure in business and he drank too much. His administration as President of the United States was not the most effective. He was not an efficient organizer and was a bit unrefined. However, history remembers him as the General who won the Civil War and preserved the Union. Why? He was a man who understood the times and knew what to do. He was a man of forceful action fitting of the moment.

The Advantages of ACTION

✓ *Breeds confidence* – Workers gather to work, not to guess, analyze, or surmise. Lack of action and the failure to prescribe something to do implies to the worker or workers that they do not possess the talent or wherewithal to tackle the challenge.

✓ *Focuses concentration* – having a task at hand makes workers prioritize and gives them the opportunity to excel. It does the same thing for you, the leader.

✓ *Builds esteem* – Action yields more action. You are, I hope, building subordinates with the capacity to handle greater responsibilities with greater independence. Competence and confidence are essential in a self-motivating self-mobilizing workforce. Prescribed action is the best training.

✓ *Economizes effort* – duplicate effort is demoralizing and defeating. Prescribed action from you the leader, who understands the times and knows what to do, creates economy of effort allowing more to be accomplished with less.

Effective leaders understand the times and know what to do next. They comprehend the demands of the circumstances and know whether to be X or Y. To make the correct decision and take the correct action is imperative.

Leadership functions most visibly in crunch time and crisis. Leadership proves itself on every level, but we most often identify it when stakes are high. Earlier I used the examples of Mayor Giuliani and Michael Vance's story of Disneyland. In both accounts it was very clear the powerful and decisive effects of ready and prompt action. But it was not just any decision or just any action.

Decisions must be made, and executed, well, decisively. When the right decision is made in a timely manner and the right action is prescribed, a symphony of successes is the result.

TAKEAWAYS

- ✓ Leadership is not a figurehead function. It must engage real life with corresponding and appropriate action.
- ✓ There are four benefits of action
  - o It breeds confidence.
  - o It focuses concentration.
  - o It builds esteem.
  - o It economizes effort.
- ✓ There are four consequences of inaction
  - o It provokes doubt.
  - o It contributes to confusion.
  - o It allows the McLellan Syndrome to set in.
  - o It breeds failure to try.

Skill #3 – Exercise The Authority To Make It Happen

> *"Leading is easy, the hard part is getting people to follow."*
>
> Yogi Berra

Ok, so you can accurately read the circumstances and the people in them, have a clear concept of what has to be done, and can confidently articulate why it needs to be done. Can you get anyone to cooperate with your plan?

In the first section of this book, I quoted a

verse from the Old Testament. I want to revisit it because it has direct relevance to this, the third skill.

*"AND OF THE SONS OF ISSACHAR, MEN WHO UNDERSTOOD THE TIMES, WITH KNOWLEDGE OF WHAT ISRAEL SHOULD DO, THEIR CHIEFS WERE TWO HUNDRED; AND ALL THEIR KINSMEN WERE AT THEIR **COMMAND**." 1 CHRONICLES 12:32*

It is the concept and practice of "command" that I want to focus on. Let me preface my explanation of this practice by defining what it is and what it is not.

- ✓ To *"Command"* is to exercise authority but not the mere manifestation of authoritarianism.

- ✓ *"Command"* is to offer direction (where we should be heading) and directions (instructions either general or specific about what to do in order to get there).

✓ *In "Command"* is to manifest a *command presence* not just bravado, bluster, or arrogance.

The capacity, the skill to command, is directly proportional to a leader's *command presence*.

Command presence is a military term which describes the respect others offer to you, the influence they allow you to have with them, and the willingness with which they will follow you. Command presence cannot be faked. You either have it or you don't.

This is not to say those you lead will not respect, respond, or follow you without it. They may do so because you occupy a formal position of leadership – your position in the company or organization which comes with a certain authority. But in the long run, over time your people will get to know you and this is where command presence dominates.

If you've watched classic American television, you have likely seen the exploits of Sheriff Andy Taylor and his intrepid deputy Barney Fife. Forgive me for using a fictitious illustration of a very real principle. Barney means well, takes his job seriously, and accepts responsibility willingly. But the badge he wears, the symbol of his authority, is not supported by a command presence.

> *Authority is delegated downward but awarded upward.*

One in a position of leadership may carry the trappings of authority bestowed upon them by the organization or company for which they work. But there is another dynamic that plays out here:

The people you lead must allow you the authority you wield. If they don't, you can carry on for a while by sheer authoritarianism, but they *will get you back.*

Command presence is the consequence of character proven over time, consistently fair treatment of subordinates, obvious knowledge proven in real life practice, and wisdom born in the fires of experience.

New followers who have not had the benefit of working with you will grant you a line of credit, so to speak. They will allow you a certain time to demonstrate your

*Effective, successful leaders have followers who are not only **willing** to be led by them, those followers are also **proud** to be led by them.*

competence and command presence and will follow you during that time. If time proves the credit they've extended to you to be a worthy investment, they will continue to willingly follow and eventually escalate their compliance into pride.

Leaders with command presence instill confidence. They never waver, never waffle, and never prevaricate. They press on, speak with certainty, issue orders with confidence, and reason persuasively.

Ask yourself this:

- ✓ When you enter a room, does anyone notice?

- ✓ When you speak does anyone listen?

- ✓ When you lead does anyone follow?

Command presence manifests itself physically by body language. Leaders with command presence stand straight, don't slouch, and dress appropriately. They use the trappings of power and authority within the context in which they function. They carry themselves with authority, not bluster. Demeanor and appearance means the person takes his responsibilities seriously and knows that dozens, perhaps many dozens of little things add up to create a package representing authority and function.

Command presence validates itself psychologically through a track record of sound decisions. Followers either see what you are doing and have done or they hear about it through others. Nothing encourages success like success.

Command presence manifests itself audibly. Leaders who possess it speak clearly, articulate their arguments, offer sound counsel, and lay out their ideas coherently. If you recall, I began this book with a reference to leadership in the Navajo tribe. I revealed that the Navajo word for leader is orator. Navajo leaders find themselves in places of power because they speak well. This factor is universally true. Leaders everywhere are articulate people, a key component of command presence.

Effective, successful leaders:

- ✓ Understand the "times."

- ✓ Know "what to do" next.

- ✓ Are able to "command" people to get things done.

Do you?

Are you "Issacharian?" How clearly do you understand the times? In the position of leadership you presently occupy, do you know what to do next? Are you able to shoulder the mantle of command effectively?

TAKEAWAYS

- ✓ The hard part is getting people to follow.
- ✓ Command presence is not bluster.
- ✓ Leaders with command presence instill confidence and evoke cooperation.
- ✓ Command presence is the consequence of character proven over time, consistently fair treatment of subordinates, obvious knowledge proven in real life practice, and wisdom born in the fires of experience.

Ending at the Beginning

In the chapters above I have referred to Mayor Giuliani's leadership on September 11th, General's Grant and McLellan as they led troops in America's Civil War, and an astute supervisor's actions on Main Street in Disneyland.

What, you may ask, does any of that have to do with me? The examples I selected are, for the most part, larger than life figures. Larger than life examples vividly demonstrate the points I want to make. Each of them in each example illustrated the three essential skills.

Here's the key: If they did, you can too. The leadership they exhibited was not the result of luck, fortune, or benevolent relatives. No one gave them positions of responsibility because they were owed favors. No, they earned those positions and, through the execution of the three skill, proved they were capable, effective leaders.

If you lead a small group or a large company, the same three skills come into play all the time. They may be most evident in times of urgency and crisis, but they are there all the time.

The Three Absolutely Necessary, Always Present Skills of an Effective, Successful Leader work everywhere every time. They are not the only skills you will need to lead successfully, but they are the first three that define and proclaim leadership. Without them, neither a great idea nor a noble vision will make it to reality.

Effective leadership is a mix of skills, attitudes, and circumstances. Most will probably find it difficult to define. On the surface this is largely true.

However, when we break it apart, study its components, its construction, and its many applications; we begin to see across the board elements appear.

In the first chapter I called these elements *principles* because they are universal and fundamental. This booklet has addressed the most primary of effective leadership principles. These three are always present and always executed well by effective, successful, and practical leaders.

But there are more; many more. Motivation, delegation, time management, vision, people skills, integrity and wholeness, adaptability, and more reside in any effective leader's toolbox.

The next book in this series – What You See is What You Get – addresses the pivotal and critical role vision plays in every leader's experience. You can download a free sample at **www.jackdunigan.com** or at the publisher's website **www.LifeMetricsMedia.com**.

Those who attend schools of leadership discover that learning does not end with the close of the class. To keep learning, I confidently invite you to become a regular visitor to

www.ThePracticalLeader.com

Quick links to purchase this book, and others, in either printed or digital versions, are found at:

www.ThePracticalLeader.com

www.JackDunigan.com

www.LifeMetricsMedia.com

Glossary

Authority: power to influence or command thought, opinion or behavior.

Command: manifest a presence of authority and influence which inspires others to listen to what you have to say and respond

Discernment: to intuit the unobvious

Dynamics: the forces, often emotional and psychological that influence a situation or group.

Insight: the ability to discern the dynamics of any given situation, setting, opportunity, and group.

Intuition: the power or faculty of knowing things without conscious reasoning. Also called discernment.

Leadership: the art and science of letting people have your own way.

Observation: to see through careful attention.

Outsight: the vision to see the end from the beginning and the steps in between.

Perception: the ability to understand

Politics: Pursuit of individual agendas and self-interest in an organization without regard to their effect on the organization's efforts to achieve its goals.

Political: the manipulation of the dynamics of self-interest and individual agendas active within other individuals or groups in order to further one's own self-interest and individual agenda.

Power: the ability to act or produce some effect.

Principle: a general truth or axiom.

Understanding: to grasp the meaning of.

Why this book is this length?

Digital media has radically changed the way information is prepared, presented, and distributed to the consumer. The manner in which readers and learners gather and process information has shaped and been shaped by the proliferation of e-readers, tablets, and smartphones. The fast pace of life has made smaller capsules of information and entertainment far more useful.

So, the trend these days is toward micro-books. At one time, a broader subject was addressed and explored in a longer and more comprehensive volume. A book of yesterday's length might take many days or weeks to digest. Today, readers and learners simply do not have the luxury to process so much information at one stretch. They want a book they can rad cover to cover on a commute.

Apple and I-tunes changed the way we buy and listen to music. If I want to hear one song, I no longer need to buy an entire album. Now I can purchase one track at a time through a number of music stores.

Well, the same principle is altering the written word too. No longer does one need to buy an entire book when all they want is the information in one or two chapters. This book is this length because I have taken what amounts to a very large body of work on the subject of effective leadership and broken it into smaller segments that relate to each other but are capable of standing alone. So, this book is this length. I hope you want the other volumes, but sincerely wish you can gather whatever you need to make your leadership experience even more effective.

Acknowledgements

It may seem out of place to insert acknowledgements at the end of the book. After all, those being acknowledged may feel slighted. Authors usually address those associates who have assisted in the creation of the manuscript in a more honorable and accessible position.

However, the location, more precisely, the relocation of acknowledgements to the back of the book is due to one thing only.

These days, most books are sold on-line, even printed volumes like this one. The internet has forced a change in the way books are marketed. Most on-line book sellers offer a glimpse inside, much the same way that street-side bookstores allow customers to browse the pages before deciding to buy. So, on-line vendors have told us that books market better when a reader can get to the meat of the manuscript early on. They tell us to place acknowledgements and anything else not directly part of the book's subject matter at the end...or omit it entirely.

I am uncomfortable enough with placing this notice back here. I am certainly not going to completely ignore those who have made this possible.

The first acknowledgement must go to my encouraging and supportive wife, Sue. She has contributed to this entire series in many ways over many years. She has sat attentively in my seminars listening to material she has heard over and over. She has offered advice about presentation and formatting. And most recently, she has functioned as chief proofreader and editor. A published author in her own right her work can be read most recently in *"Chicken Soup for the Soul: Moms Know Best."* (Available at Amazon, Barnes & Noble, and other book sellers.)

Next will be those who have helped shape my thinking through the years, the number of them is legion. I will spare the reader the list of those who demonstrated all too clearly how to lead really badly. I learned a good deal from them, or maybe in spite of them, but their existence deserves a nod.

The most consistently positive example of effective leadership is David Fritsche, Sr., whose lifelong manifestation of effectiveness has made a lasting impression not only in the region in which he has worked but much, much farther.

So, to all of you, my appreciation!

Find out more about leadership, business, and successful living at my blogs and websites below. At each you will find an opportunity to sign up for a free newsletter. When you sign up you will receive regular updates, advance notice of new books, and important information about your profession or industry.

www.ThePracticalLeader.com

www.DuniganReport.com

www.TheSavvyWoodworker.com

www.JackDunigan.com

www.Aidchild.org
(This is a cause I fully support and believe in.)

Videos are available free of charge on my YouTube channels. Links are on each of the websites above, or just search YouTube for Jack Dunigan.

24064947R00052

Printed in Great Britain
by Amazon